# WORLD OF KNOWLEDGE

# The Human World

**PhP**

PETER HADDOCK PUBLISHING

Text by Meme Ltd, ©PHP.

# Contents

**Photo credits:** Jupiter Images: 1, 2, 4, 5 top, 6 bottom, 7, 8, 9, 10, 11, 12, 13 top, 15, 16, 17, 18, 19 top, 20, 21 bottom, 22 bottom, 25 bottom, 26, 27 top and middle, 28, 29, 30, 31 bottom, 33, 34 bottom, 35, 36, 37, 38, 39 bottom, 40, 43 bottom, 44 bottom, 45 bottom. Photodisc: 3, 24 top. Hemera Images: 14 bottom, 41. NASA: 19 bottom. US Marine Corps: 22 middle. US Navy: 23. USAF: 25 top. US Library of Congress: 31 top.

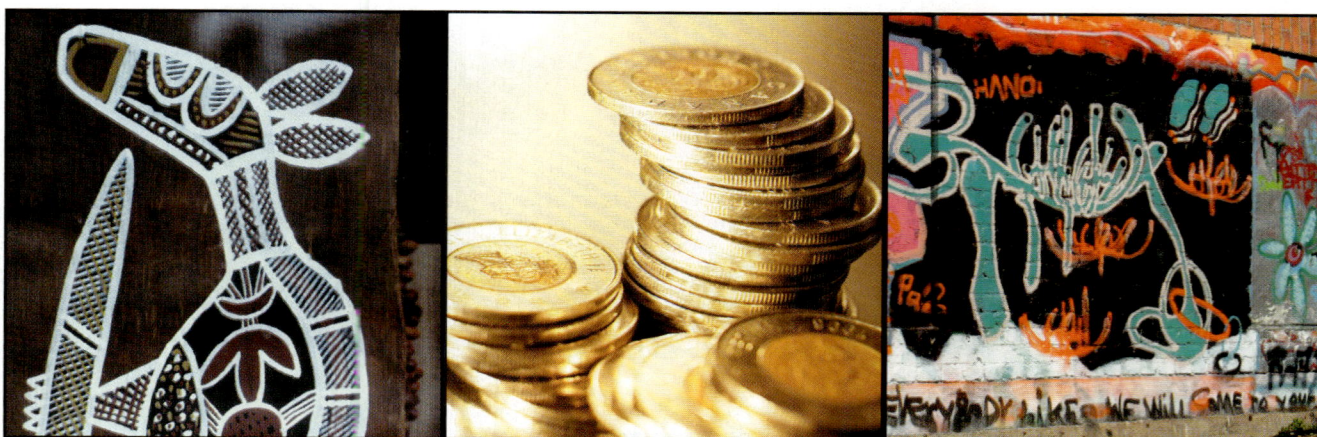

# Introduction

The Human World is our world, as rich in diversity as we are ourselves. But where did we come from, where are we going and how are we going to get there?

To understand who we are, we need to be able to look at our past. We also need to look at how we are now and appreciate the diversity that we have achieved. A journey through our world will show just how remarkable our achievements are and just how much has been accomplished by people in the last 4,000 years of recorded history.

A tiny step in geological time has seen the human race leap from Stone Aged cave dweller to masters of technology, who are on the verge of leaving our planet for a life in the stars. With so much progress packed into the last 4,000 years, no one can know where we will be in 4,000 years' time.

How many of our customs, our art and literature will we have taken with us? Will we indeed still be human?

# Culture and Customs

Tallest, fattest, cleverest, richest, poorest. We love facts, but most of all we love facts about other people, particularly the weird and wonderful.

# Which is the world's oldest culture?

Australia's aboriginal culture is the oldest continuous living culture in the world. It dates back between 40,000 and 60,000 years, and may be even older. Aborigines have a great respect for, and belief in, nature. They lived as nomads, living off the land by following the seasons and the food. Aborigines passed on stories of creation, laws and trading routes through stories, dancing and painting. Stories called 'The Dreaming' tell of the journey and actions of beings that created the natural world, and are an important part of aboriginal culture.

Aborigines believe in ancestor worship. The spirits of their dead ancestors inhabit the sacred places of their land. Aborigines commune with these spirits in order to seek advice. Their culture has also produced the striking art forms that they are famous for. Aboriginal art is highly symbolic. They believe that in some way the image of an animal is part of the actual animal.

*Uluru (Ayres Rock) is one of the Aborigines' most sacred sites. It was handed back to them in the 1980s. Despite Aborigines' protests, tourists can still climb the rock.*

## Who are the Bedouins?

Bedouins are nomadic people from the Middle East and North Africa. The word Bedouin means 'desert dweller'. Bedouins herd camels, sheep, horses, donkeys and goats and move with the seasons to find grazing and water for their animals. They travel in tribes of extended families. The head of the tribe is a sheik. They live in tents which enables them to move around easily and are famous for their hospitality. The Bedouin way of life has been threatened by modern culture, and the numbers of Bedouins have decreased in recent years.

## What is the Japanese tea ceremony?

The Japanese tea ceremony is a traditional way of making and serving green tea. It is known as chado or sado, which means 'the way of tea'. The rituals of the tea ceremony have to be learned by heart, and many Japanese go to tea ceremony classes to learn the art. Everything that is used in the tea ceremony has meaning, including the tools that are used to make the tea as well as the art that is hanging on the wall. Chado is closely linked to Buddhism, and it is believed that one should always perform the best ceremony possible as each meeting will only happen once and can never be repeated.

## How many languages are there in the world?

No one can know for sure how many languages are spoken all over the world. Many are spoken by only a few people in very remote parts of the world. The United Nations recognises 6,912 living languages, of which 2,261 have writing systems. While this shows that most languages are spoken only, these are all very minor languages. A language is said to be living if it is still spoken in daily use and is still evolving and changing. Dead languages are ones that either have no living speakers or have ceased to evolve. Latin is spoken by many people but is regarded as a dead language as no new words are being added to it. Similarly languages such as Scottish Gaelic are still spoken but new words and phrases tend to be taken from modern English.

## How do the Inuits of Greenland survive in their freezing environment?

The temperatures in Greenland can fall to as low as −500˚C. Frostbite and hypothermia are great risks to people living in the extreme cold. Warm clothes are essential to protect against the cold. Animal skins, such as seal, caribou and polar bear are worn in layers which help trap the heat. The inner layer would have the fur next to the skin and the outer layer would have the fur on the outside. Women make a lot of the clothes, chewing the skins to soften it and then sewing tight stitches to make it waterproof. Inuits always cover their heads as a lot of heat is lost through the head. Stockings are made from hareskin and waterproof boots from sealskin. Although many Inuits wear modern clothing at home they still wear traditional clothing when out hunting.

# What is the Chinese zodiac?

The Chinese zodiac is a 12-year cycle represented by animals. The beginning of the year is between the end of January and the beginning of February, depending on the cycles of the moon. Each year is given an animal sign which is repeated every 12 years: rat, ox, tiger, rabbit, dragon, snake, horse, sheep, monkey, rooster, dog and boar.

The Chinese believe that the sign you are born under has great bearing on what sort of person you are and your chances of a successful and lucky life. The signs also provide an easy way of finding out how old someone is by asking what their animal sign is. 9 February 2005 to 28 January 2006 is the year of the rooster.

The Chinese Lunar Calendar names each of the 12 years after an animal. Legend has it that the Lord Buddha summoned all the animals to come to him before he departed from Earth. Only 12 came to bid him farewell and as a reward he named a year after each one in the order they arrived. The Chinese believe the animal ruling the year in which a person is born has a profound influence on personality, saying: 'This is the animal that hides in your heart.'

**Which animal are you? Look up your birthday to find out.**

| Rat | 1924 | 1936 | 1948 | 1960 | 1972 | 1984 | 1996 |
|---|---|---|---|---|---|---|---|
| Ox | 1925 | 1937 | 1949 | 1961 | 1973 | 1985 | 1997 |
| Tiger | 1926 | 1938 | 1950 | 1962 | 1974 | 1986 | 1998 |
| Rabbit | 1927 | 1939 | 1951 | 1963 | 1975 | 1987 | 1999 |
| Dragon | 1928 | 1940 | 1952 | 1964 | 1976 | 1988 | 2000 |
| Snake | 1929 | 1941 | 1953 | 1965 | 1977 | 1989 | 2001 |
| Horse | 1930 | 1942 | 1954 | 1966 | 1978 | 1990 | 2002 |
| Sheep | 1931 | 1943 | 1955 | 1967 | 1979 | 1991 | 2003 |
| Monkey | 1932 | 1944 | 1956 | 1968 | 1980 | 1992 | 2004 |
| Rooster | 1933 | 1945 | 1957 | 1969 | 1981 | 1993 | 2005 |
| Dog | 1934 | 1946 | 1958 | 1970 | 1982 | 1994 | 2006 |
| Boar | 1935 | 1947 | 1959 | 1971 | 1983 | 1995 | 2007 |

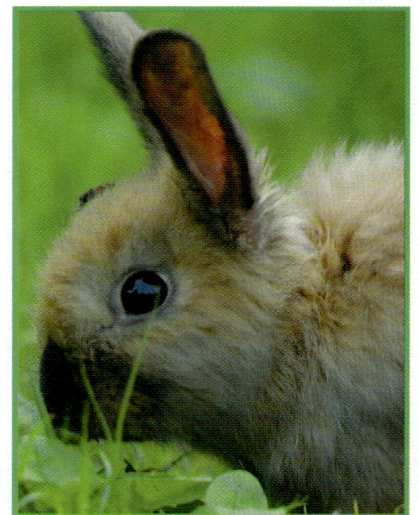

## What is a bar mitzvah?

Bar mitzvah is the Jewish coming of age ceremony. A boy undergoes his bar mitzvah when he turns 13. Girls undergo a similar ceremony called a bat mitzvah when they are 12, although reformed Jews celebrate both coming of ages at 13.

Upon celebrating their coming of age, a child is considered to have become an adult in the eyes of Jewish law. They are now responsible for their own actions spiritually, ethically and morally.

This turning point is marked by celebrations both in the synagogue and at home. The celebrations welcome the former child into the adult world and encourage them to take their place in the adult Jewish community. The celebrations can often be very lavish with gifts and money being bestowed on the person being bar mitzvahed.

## What is Halloween?

Halloween is a festival celebrated in many western countries, but mostly in America. It is closely associated with ghostly goings on and people enjoy dressing up as witches and ghouls, as well as watching horror movies and telling ghost stories. People go from door to door in a custom called 'Trick or Treating' where householders give the visitors treats in order to prevent them performing some trick on them. At this time of year pumpkins are plentiful and people carve them into lanterns that they carry or display in windows.

The festival started out as the Christian 'All Hallows Even'. The celebration day became associated with the ancient Celtic end of summer called Samhain (pronounced Sowen). One story says that, on that day, the disembodied spirits of all those who had died throughout the preceding year would come back in search of living bodies to possess for the next year. It was believed to be their only hope for the afterlife. The Celts believed all laws of space and time were suspended during this time, allowing the spirit world to intermingle with the living.

## Do Mormons really have more than one wife?

The practice of having more than one wife is called polygamy. Many ancient cultures practised polygamy as the number of wives a man could support was a show of his wealth and power. Gradually this practice has become rarer, and indeed is illegal in most western countries as it is unfair to the women involved. Mormons (a religious group from Utah in the USA) are famous for having more than one wife, however, this is not true. The Mormon Church specifically forbids its members from having more than one wife. This led to some members leaving the church and setting up their own group, called the Splendors that does allow polygamy. Polygamy itself is illegal in America and several ex-Mormons have been jailed for having more than one wife.

## Who are the Amish?

The Amish are a community in America. They live mostly in Pennsylvania. The Amish live by a strict code that forbids most of the technology of our modern world. The Amish are particularly against technology that connects them to the outside world such as the telephone and mains electricity. They are the descendants of original Dutch settlers and most still speak a language called Pennsylvania Dutch or German. The Amish dress and live simple lives and use horses in preference to cars. As a result of their self-sufficient lifestyle they are mostly farmers. Their lifestyle is seen as idyllic by many people but their close-knit communities suffer from many social problems and women and children can suffer as a result.

## What are vegetarians and vegans?

Some people believe that it is wrong to breed and kill animals simply to eat them. These people do not eat meat and are called vegetarians. Some vegetarians eat fish but most do not. Vegetarians replace the meat in their diet with pulses such as lentils and nuts. Vegans are similar to vegetarians but their dietary rules are much more strict. They will not eat foods that contain animal by-products. This means they do not eat cheese as it contains rennet, or milk as it comes from a cow, rather they drink soya milk and special rennet-free cheeses. They do not wear animal products either, so they will not buy leather shoes. Products, such as wool, that do not harm the animal are permitted.

*Fish and chips is the most popular way that most people eat fish. The busiest day in a chip shop is Friday.*

## Why do we eat fish on Fridays?

This is a remnant of more strict Catholic times. Originally Christians were instructed not to eat meat on Fridays. Fish was not regarded as meat so people ate that instead. Despite the many years since this has been a requirement, people still eat more fish on Fridays than any other day. Other religions still have strict dietary requirements. Jewish people are forbidden from eating pork, while Muslims must only eat meat that has been produced using strict guidelines. Such meat is called Halal meat.

11

# Inventions

Inventions, a testimony to the creative power of the human mind. No sooner does an opportunity arise than someone has invented the answer, often to a question we have not yet asked.

## Who invented paper money?

The Chinese were the first people to use paper money, around 800 AD. It was called 'flying money' because it was so light that the wind could blow it away. This first money was more like an 'IOU' note – people could deposit coins in exchange for a piece of paper, which they could then exchange back into coins elsewhere. By 1294 silk notes had taken over as the currency all over China and Persia. In 1375 the first paper note was issued, called the 'Precious Note of Great Ming'. There was only one denomination for 200 years, and change was given with coins. The first paper money in the West was introduced by Sweden in 1661. Now every country in the world uses paper money.

## What's in YOUR pocket?

Different countries use different currencies. The most popular names for money are dollar, pound and euro, which are all used by many different countries. Some countries, however, like to use something different. In Thailand they have the bart, in Costa Rica it's the colon, in Haiti they spend gourdes, in Poland they use the zloty and in Malaysia they use ringgits!

## Who invented the wheel?

The wheel is one of the greatest inventions in the world. They are used not only for transport but also in machines, generators for electricity and in watches that tell us the time. The first wheel was probably invented around 8000 BC in Asia, although the first known wheel was made around 3500 BC by the Sumerians in Mesopotamia (modern Iraq) from solid wood. They used large four-wheeled carts to carry heavy items such as metal, wood and army supplies. Some other uses for wheels include making pottery and grindstones. About 1,000 years later, the Egyptians improved the wheel by adding spokes. The wheel began to be used around the ancient world, including India, Greece and Rome.

## What did Archimedes invent?

Archimedes was an inventor, mathematician and scientist. He was born in 287 BC in Syracuse, a Greek city. He invented many things, including pi (a way of calculating areas and volumes), the lever and pulley, the Archimedes screw and catapults. One of his most famous discoveries was why some objects float and others sink. When getting into his bath one day he noticed that his body caused the water level to rise. He was so excited that he jumped out of the bath and ran naked down the street shouting, 'Eureka, eureka!' which means 'I have found it'. He was killed in 212 BC when the Romans invaded his city.

## When were balloons invented?

Balloons were invented in England in 1824. The first balloons were made from pigs' bladders and then later from rubber. Modern balloons, made from latex (the milky sap from rubber trees), were invented by an American, Neil Tillotson in 1931. While attempting to make an inner tube from latex, he drew a cat's head on a piece of cardboard and dipped it in latex. When it dried he blew it up and was amazed that he had a cat balloon, complete with ears. He made 2,000 balloons and sold them on the street during the annual parade day. They were so popular that he set up his own balloon manufacturing company.

# When was Morse code invented?

Morse code was invented in 1837 by an American, Samuel Morse, who was born in 1791. It was a code that used dots and dashes to represent the letters of the alphabet. A key was tapped to send messages. The code was transmitted by electric wire, allowing people in different places to communicate instantly for the first time. The first telegraph line between two cities was constructed in 1844 between Baltimore and Washington, and the first message 'What hath God wrought' was tapped out. Morse code was also used in World War Two to signal with flashes of light. Since World War Two, there has only been one new addition to the Morse Code. This being the '@' symbol which was added in December 2003.

# Who invented Braille?

Braille was invented by a French boy, Louis Braille, who was born in 1809. He had become blind after an accident when he was three years old. While at school in Paris, a captain from the French army, Charles Barbier de la Serre, visited the school to show them his invention that used raised dots which could be read in the dark. It turned out to be not very useful for the army as it was too bulky, but he hoped that it might be of use to blind people. At the age of 15 years, Louis adapted this method and reduced the number of dots used to make the method simpler to read. He used six dots instead of the 12 dots that Barbier used, in two rows of three, which allowed blind people to read much more quickly. Louis carried on working on his invention, and developed codes for maths and music.

## Who invented the light bulb?

The first electric light was produced in 1800 by a scientist from England, Humphry Davy, when he invented the electric battery. In 1854 a German watchmaker, Henricg Globel, invented the first proper light bulb with a bamboo filament in a glass bulb. Other people improved on Davy's invention including Joseph Swan from England who produced electric lamps in 1860, and Charles Brush from America who invented electric street lights. However, it is Thomas Edison, an inventor from America, who is best known for inventing long-lasting light bulbs in 1879. For the first time electric light was safe, cheap and practical for home use.

## Who invented sandwiches?

The first recorded sandwich was eaten by a rabbi, Hillel the Elder, in the 1st Century BC. He was the first person to put a filling between two pieces of matzos, which became the custom to eat at Passover. The modern sandwich was invented by the 4th Earl of Sandwich, John Montagu. One day in 1762, the gambler Montagu asked for some meat between two pieces of bread as he didn't want to leave the gambling table. Other people began to order 'the same as Sandwich', and the name 'sandwich' was coined.

## When were jigsaw puzzles invented?

Jigsaw puzzles were invented in 1767 by John Spilsbury, an engraver from England. He stuck the map of the world onto a piece of wood, then cut out each country. The maps were used in schools to help children learn geography. Wooden puzzles were very expensive to buy, and only the rich could afford them. But once the first cardboard puzzles were produced in the early 1900s, they became much cheaper to produce and puzzling became very popular. At first puzzles were produced mainly for children, but by 1900 they became popular with adults too. These early puzzles were very difficult, with pieces that did not interlock and no picture on the box to provide a guide. Puzzles still provide entertainment and education to people of all ages to this day.

## Who invented toothbrushes?

The first 'toothbrushes' were used 5,000 years ago and were made from frayed twigs which were rubbed on the teeth to clean them. The first toothbrush was made for the Emperor of China in 1498. It was made from the bristles of a pig embedded in a bone handle. In 1770 a British prisoner, William Addis, had the idea of placing bristles into holes in a bone, which he glued into place. When he was released from prison he started up a business mass-producing toothbrushes. In 1938 nylon bristles were first produced. The first electric toothbrush was developed in 1939 in Switzerland.

## How was plastic invented?

The first plastic was called Parkesine and was discovered in 1862 by Alexander Parkes, a British inventor. Parkesine was made from the cellulose of plants with added chemicals. The first completely synthetic plastic, known as Bakelite, was made by an American chemist, Leo Baekeland. He called it 'the material of a thousand uses', and it was soon used for electrical insulation, radios, toilet seats, ashtrays and telephones. Another American chemist, Waldo Semon, accidentally discovered PVC (polyvinyl chloride) in 1929. The new material was soon used to make many new products, such as hosepipes and records. Today, plastics are everywhere and part of our everyday life and are used to make thousands of items from toys to bottles to sports equipment.

## The problem with plastic

Plastic is so useful and used by us in so many ways that is difficult to understand how damaging it is to the environment. Modern plastics are a product of the petro-chemical industry. It is made from the same materials as the fuel in our cars. Plastic is made from some very hardwearing molecules. Once made, it stays made, often for many thousands of years. Most plastic ends up in landfill sites where it just sits there. It is possible to make plastic that decomposes when exposed to sunlight, unfortunately most of it still ends up in the landfill, where it is quickly covered up, away from the light. The best solution is to use less plastic. This means using paper bags at the supermarket and choosing food packaged in glass or other environmentally friendly materials.

*The cheapness and availability of plastic has made many items disposable. Years ago this bucket and spade set would have been made from metal and wood, both of which decompose.*

## How did computers begin?

Basic machines for calculating have been around for thousands of years since the Babylonians invented the abacus in 3,000 BC. The father of the computer is generally regarded as Charles Babbage. He invented what he called his difference engine. It used a series of cogs and gears to do complex calculations. Unfortunately Babbage was ahead of his time as the construction of his machines was too hard for watchmakers of his day. The dream of a computer that could be programmed to do any task was first realised by the British mathematician Alan Turing, famous as a World War Two code breaker. He theorised about a machine that could solve any problem that was solvable. Gradually, electronic computers began to evolve. One of the first 'modern' computers was ENIAC – the Electronic Numerical Integrator and Calculator. It was designed in 1945. This huge machine took up a whole room and needed its own air conditioner to keep it cool. It could add about 5,000 numbers a second. By the 1960s computers were getting more and more powerful but they still filled rooms. In 1981 IBM introduced the first desktop PC using Microsoft BASIC. From that point computers have become faster and faster. The slowest desktop machines now routinely operate at over 10 billion calculations a second.

## When was the telephone invented?

In America in 1876 two men, Elisha Gray and Alexander Graham Bell, both invented telephones independently of each other. Bell managed to get his invention to the patent office just two hours before Gray, and so became known as the inventor of the telephone. The Bell Telephone Company was founded, and became the largest telephone company in the world. The first phone call was made by Bell to his assistant in the next room saying 'Come here, Watson, I want you'. The first telephone exchange was built in Connecticut in 1877. Early exchanges needed operators to connect calls manually. These days exchanges are controlled by computers and the phone network is the most complicated machine on the planet.

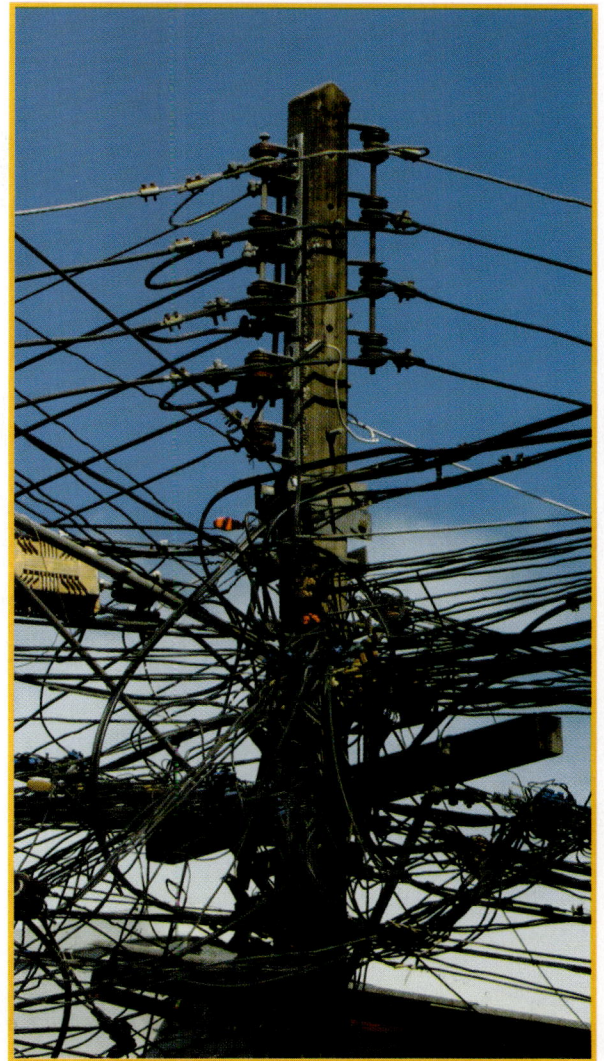

# War and Conflict

War. The result of our worst animal instincts. The 20th Century saw more people killed in war than the rest of human history combined. The 21st Century can only get better.

THE GREAT WAR FOR CIVILISATION 1914-1919

# What started the First World War?

World War One began on 28 June 1914. It was sparked by the assassination of Archduke Franz Ferdinand of Austria by a Serbian student Gavrilo Princip in Bosnia. As a result Austro-Hungary declared war on Serbia, and Germany declared war on Russia who had joined forces with Serbia. Germany then invaded France, and Britain declared war on Germany, and Austro-Hungary declared war on Britain. In all, 35 nations were involved in the war. The war ended just over four years later on 11 November 1918. It is estimated that 15 million people died during the war.

*World War One saw the introduction of trench warfare and industrial killing. Millions died.*

# How many people were killed in the Second World War?

*A B-17 bomber from World War Two. This war saw the introduction of mass bombing of both military and civilian targets. It was the first war where the people back at home suffered as much as the troops at the front line and is one of the reasons that the death toll was so high.*

More people were killed in World War Two than in any other war – around 50 million people lost their lives. The war began on 3 September 1939 and ended in 1945. It was fought on the land, in the air and on the seas. More advanced technology and the development of weapons such as bombs, tanks, submarines and poisonous gas resulted in a huge death toll. Two atomic bombs were dropped in Japan at the end of the war. The first, in Hiroshima, killed more than 140,000 people. Three days later another bomb was dropped on Nagasaki, killing more than 70,000 people.

## Who invented the tank?

Tanks were invented by the British army towards the end of World War One. Early tanks were slow and unreliable but effective. Soon after their introduction the German army began to produce its own tanks but they were too late to make any difference to the outcome of the war. Tanks came

into their own in World War Two when the German army invented the Blitzkrieg (Lightning War), where fast, light tanks raced ahead of the soldiers to destroy the enemy. Modern tanks are huge, complex machines weighing up to 60 tons. They are heavily armoured and have guns that can fire accurately over several miles even when the tank is moving. The two best tanks in the world are the British Challenger 2 and the American Abrams M1A2.

## How did guns change the course of war?

For thousands of years, wars had been fought with swords with enemies in close proximity. However, the invention of the gun changed all that. Guns allowed men to fight from a distance. The rapid-fire gun, or machine gun, was developed during the American Civil War. It revolutionised war still further, as many bullets could be fired each minute. The change brought about by machine guns was so great that it took generals many years to work out how to fight against an enemy equipped with them. The trenches of the First World War and the huge casualties were brought about mostly by armies trying to adapt old fighting methods to the new weapons. Today soldiers are far more mobile than they used to be as they need to be able to fight and move quickly in order to avoid enemy machine guns.

## Which weapons are used underwater?

Submarines are the navy's hidden weapons. They cruise under the water and are used for both defence and attack. Submarines carry a wide range of weapons including torpedoes and missiles for use against ships or land targets. Some submarines, called SNMBs, carry nuclear warheads aimed at potential enemy targets. Others are used to hunt other submarines which they attack using homing torpedoes. These subs also attack surface ships with missiles. Ships use underwater bombs called depth charges to defend themselves. These are launched from either the deck of the ship or dropped from helicopters.

## How do cruise missiles work?

Cruise missiles are weapons that look like small planes but have no pilot. The missile is about 6m long and travels at a speed of around 900kph. Missiles may be fired from land or submarines at sea. They are aimed at targets a long way away. The Tomahawk cruise missile can target a car 1,600km away. They are launched using a booster rocket. The missiles are guided by computers and a large bomb is detonated when it hits the target. They fly fast at low altitude, allowing them to avoid radar detection. Once launched, cruise missiles are virtually impossible to stop as they are small and are often launched in groups.

## What are atomic bombs?

Atomic bombs are nuclear bombs that use uranium to create a blast that is far bigger than conventional explosives. The explosion from an atomic bomb is deadly. The initial explosion causes a huge fireball that will destroy anything within 2km of the centre of the blast (called ground zero). This huge explosion also produces a wind blast that can cause concrete buildings to collapse up to 10km away. A mushroom cloud of poisonous gases develops over the area hit, and can rise many kilometres into the air. Those who are not killed in the initial blast are subject to radioactive poisoning from the rain that follows which is full of radioactive particles. Many suffer from leukemia and other cancers. It also affects future generations of those that survive – leukemia is often passed on to their children. Two atomic bombs have been dropped during war – both of them in Japan at the end of World War Two. The effect was so horrific that the Japanese immediately surrendered and no nuclear weapons have been used in war since.

## The effects of an atomic bomb

This diagram shows the range at which the various effects of a 25 megaton atomic bomb blast can be felt.
Atomic bombs are unique in that the effects of their use go far beyond the initial explosion. As well as cancers caused by the exposure to lethal radiation, a nuclear war would alter the climate of the whole world, leading to what is known as a nuclear winter. This would almost certainly mean the extinction of the human race.

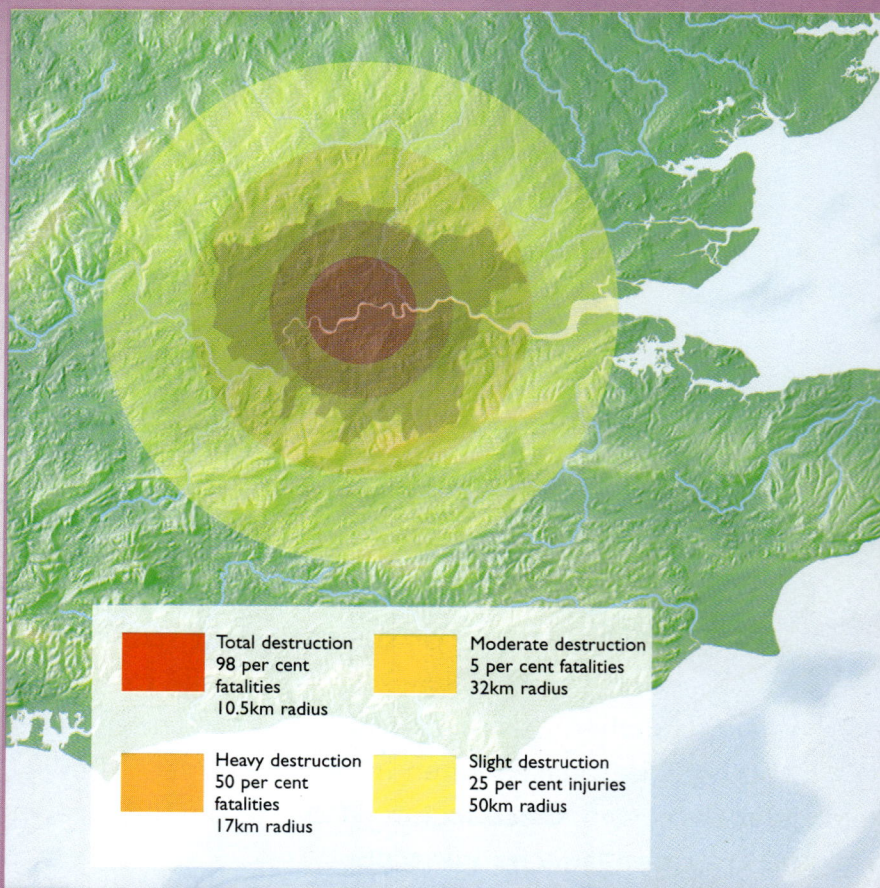

Total destruction 98 per cent fatalities 10.5km radius

Moderate destruction 5 per cent fatalities 32km radius

Heavy destruction 50 per cent fatalities 17km radius

Slight destruction 25 per cent injuries 50km radius

## How do smart bombs work?

The latest smart bombs, called Joint Direct Attack Munition, or JDAM, use satellites to guide them to their target. Smart bombs are guided to their target by Global Positioning Satellites (GPS). The position of the target is programmed into a GPS receiver in the bomb. The receiver tells the bomb where it is and where it is supposed to go to. The bomb can hit within 90cm of the target, and then explodes.

*A US Airforce crewman loads a JDAM bomb onto a strike aircraft. The US is one of only a few countries with smart weapons' technology, which gives them a decisive advantage in combat.*

## What are nerve agents?

Nerve agents are poisons that affect the nervous system. They are breathed in or absorbed through the skin. They are similar to insecticides that cause a variety of reactions, including tight chest, sweating, nausea and vomiting, convulsions, paralysis and death. The chemicals can cause death in just a few minutes. The first nerve agent, called Tabun, was made by the Germans in 1936 but not used. Nerve agents are impossible to detect in the air as they are clear and colourless and have little or no smell. Nerve agents can be spread using bombs, rockets, landmines, missiles and spray tanks.

## What was trench warfare?

When World War One started, both sides believed that they would quickly overcome the enemy and that the war would be short. However, the invention of more efficient weapons, principally the machine gun, meant that old-fashioned tactics no longer worked. Both sides quickly became unable to advance. In order to protect the troops from shelling and machine gun fire both sides constructed a system of trenches that stretched across the whole front line.

Soldiers lived in these trenches for months at a time and they quickly became full of mud and disease. Attacking the enemy was known as 'going over the top' and meant crossing a wide stretch of land between the trenches. Hundreds of thousands of men were killed doing this, often only to advance a few hundred metres.

Eventually the invention of the tank broke this deadlock and allowed the Allies to resume the attack and win the war.

## What is shell shock?

Soldiers receive a lot of training in order to ensure that they can cope with the stress of battle. However, sometimes, the strain can still become too much. During World War One the constant bombardment from artillery would reduce soldiers to nervous wrecks and they became unable to fight. Initially the officers of both sides regarded these men as cowards and many were executed for failing to follow orders. Gradually doctors realised that the men were suffering from what became known as shell shock, and began to treat them with rest and medication. Eventually many were able to return to the front line. The comedian and writer Spike Milligan suffered from shell shock during World War Two. He wrote about its effects in several books and continued to suffer from depression as a result until his death in 2002. Modern soldiers also suffer from this problem.

Today it is known as Post Traumatic Stress Disorder which is suffered as a result of the situations soldiers find themselves in and the actions they are required to perform.

# What is guerilla warfare?

Traditional armies fight each other on a battlefield. Guerilla warfare is different. When one side is much smaller and weaker than the other, fighting a traditional battle would be useless. Instead the soldiers spread out throughout the countryside, living off the land. They attack the enemy, often behind the front line, and then melt away into the countryside. Guerilla warfare is difficult to combat as the guerillas can look much like the civilian population. If the guerillas have the support of the locals then they will often grow strong enough to ensure that the invading army cannot win. Armies have found that the best way to beat guerillas is to win the support of the local population and turn them against the guerillas.

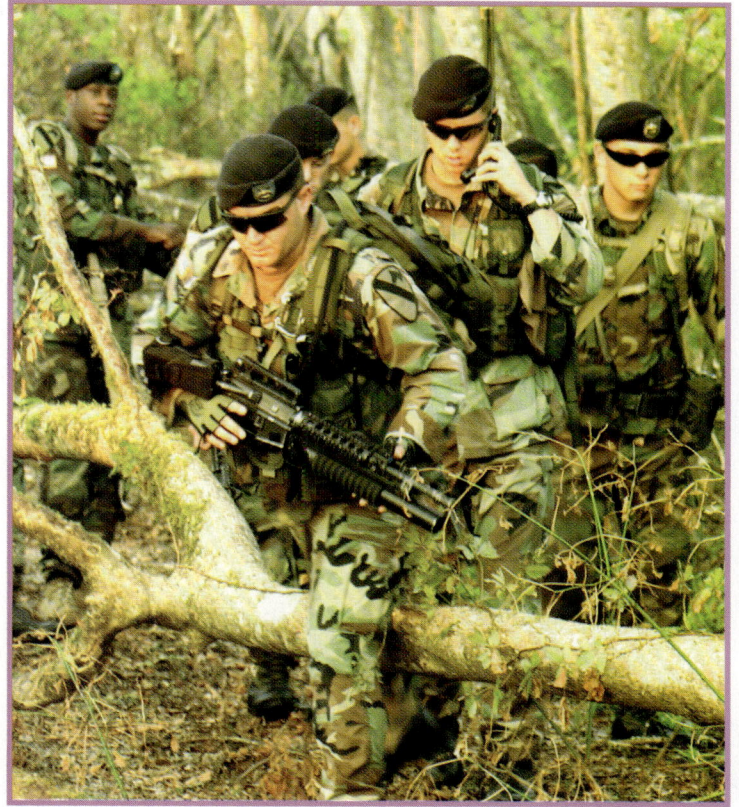

# What was the Battle of Britain?

During the early stages of World War Two, after France had surrendered, the German army was ready to invade Britain. In order to do this they had to cross the English Channel, which meant that the German airforce (the Luftwaffe) had to defeat the British airforce (the RAF). The Luftwaffe was much larger than the RAF, with many more bombers and fighters. The RAF was operating over home soil and although smaller had two very good fighters, the Supermarine Spitfire and the Hawker Hurricane. During the summer of 1940 the two sides fought a desperate battle in the air. The pilots of the RAF suffered heavy losses and the life expectancy of a new pilot was very short. Despite this, and thanks to some tactical mistakes by the German generals, the fighters of the RAF managed to defeat the Luftwaffe. Without air superiority the German army could not invade and Britain was saved. During the battle the RAF lost 1,547 aircarft while the Luftwaffe lost 1,887.

*An RAF Spitfire (above) and a Luftwaffe Focke Wulf 190E (left).*

Trade is the grease that keeps our modern world moving. We have created a complex system of trade. Whether this system is fair to all on the planet is becoming a subject for debate, trade is good for some but fair trade should be good for all.

# Trade and Commerce

## When was money invented?

The first 'money' ever used was traded for goods as long ago as 9000 BC. Cowrie shells have been used for money for thousands of years, dating back to 1200 BC when they were used in China, right up until the mid-1900s when they were still used in some parts of Africa. The first coins were invented in Lydia, Asia in 687 BC. They were made of electrum, an amalgam of gold and silver.

## Which is the most traded commodity?

Water is the most traded commodity in the world. Water is needed to produce most things, including food, computers and car components. The amount of water that is contained in and used to produce products is called virtual water. It is estimated that 1,200 litres of virtual water is needed to produce just 1kg of wheat. The US exports the largest amounts of virtual water in the world. The second most traded commodity is oil, while coffee comes in third.

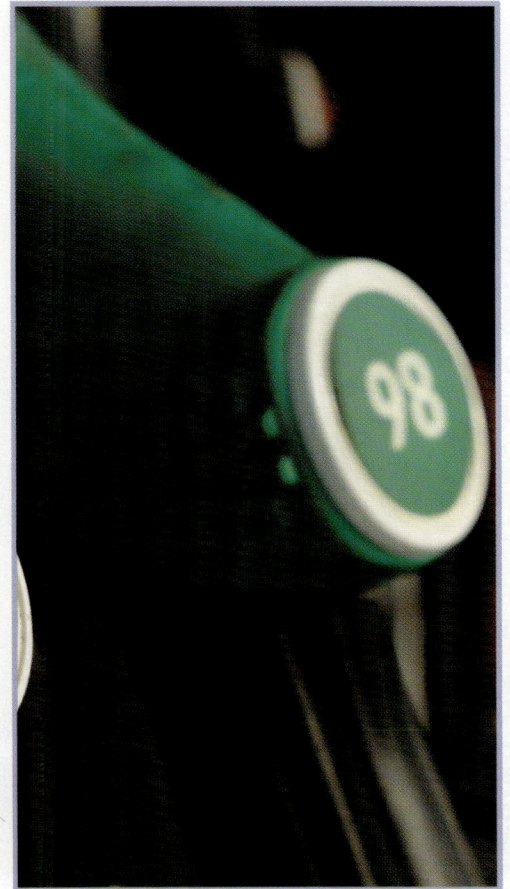

## What is fair trade?

Fair trade refers to a partnership between the growers and producers of a commodity and companies. The companies agree a fair market price for a commodity so that the growers and producers can sustain and improve their way of life. Fair trade aims to help poor and developing countries to compete in the international market. It is most often associated with coffee, but may include any goods. Workers often form cooperatives, where they band together to reduce costs and provide health care and access to loans. A large proportion of the profit made from selling goods is returned to the producer.

## What is a stock exchange?

A stock exchange is an organised market place where shares and other stocks are bought and sold. Shares are used to buy a proportion of a company. Members can buy or sell for themselves or act as agents for customers. The agent, or broker, takes a commission by charging a percentage of the stocks or shares that he or she has bought or sold. The London Stock Exchange and New York Stock Exchange are large international stock exchanges. Stock exchanges used to be noisy, crowded places as people jostled to buy and sell at the best price. Nowadays the buying and selling is done by computer. The traders in stocks and shares take a small portion of each trade they make as a commission. These small amounts can add up to large amounts and many traders become very wealthy.

## What are stocks and shares?

Stocks is the word used to describe the shares of any company, particularly more than one company, while shares refers to the stock of one particular company. Companies issue shares in order to raise money that the company needs in order to grow. When people buy shares in a company they give their money to that company. They hope that as the company grows the shares will become worth more money so that when they sell them to another person they will get back more money than they paid for them. If the company does not grow, or loses money, the shares become worthless. Shareholders own the company so they can have a say in how it is run. If the company is not run well, the shareholders will change the people who run it.

*People with no jobs or money could join government work programmes.*

## What was the Great Depression?

The Great Depression was a massive economic recession in the industrialised world that began in 1929 and lasted until 1941. It began with the crash of the New York Stock Exchange and was the longest and worst depression ever experienced in the West. Millions of people were unemployed, and many businesses became bankrupt. Thousands of people lost their life savings. In America, not only did people suffer from the depression, but a drought in the Midwest reduced the supply of food still further and many people committed suicide or starved. World War Two and military spending restarted the world economy, with many people employed in manufacturing war products or employed directly in the war.

# Why was the trade of ivory banned?

The trade of ivory was banned in 1989. Elephants have become an endangered species after years of being hunted for their ivory tusks. During the 1970s the price of ivory increased and new techniques that allowed for the mass production of ivory products increased demand. Ivory is used for jewellery and statues. In 1997 there was a partial lifting of the ban which resulted in an increase in the number of elephants killed by poachers. When the ban came into force in 1989 there were an estimated 600,000 elephants in Africa, which was down from 1.3 million in 1979. The latest figures show that the population is now only 400,000.

# What was the Silk Road?

The Silk Road was an 11,000km route that connected China to Europe, much of it through the inhospitable Taklamakan desert. The route was used from around 100 BC until the 1500s. Although silk was one of the main commodities, other products such as gold, ivory and animals were also traded. As most traders did not travel all the way along the route, but exchanged their goods fairly close to home, goods were exchanged many times along the route. The route was not one single road, but several routes, all starting from the ancient city of X'ian. The Silk Road led not only to the exchange of goods, but also the spread of ideas, cultures and religion. Sea trade and the Black Death, a disease which killed two-thirds of the population of China and millions of others in Asia and Europe, led to the decline of the route.

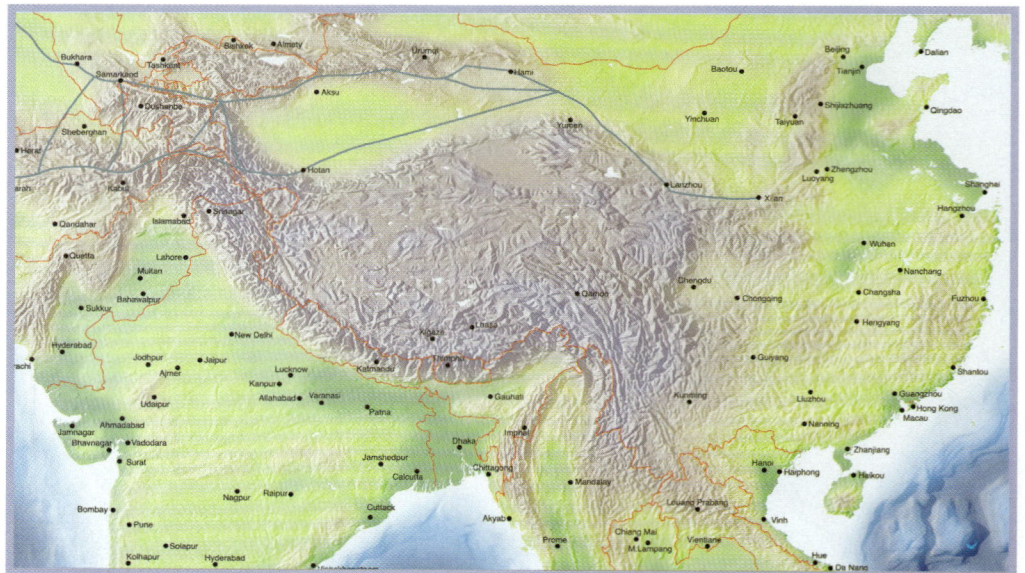

# What is a free trade area?

Normally countries compete with each other for trade. They often tax goods and services that come in from other countries in order to protect workers in their own country. However, sometimes countries agree to work together and trade between them becomes easier. These groups of countries are called free trade areas. The largest free trade areas are the European Union and The United States, Canada and Mexico. Free trade areas allow countries to work together to promote all of the members. They also allow smaller countries like Luxembourg (in Europe) to compete with larger economies more fairly.

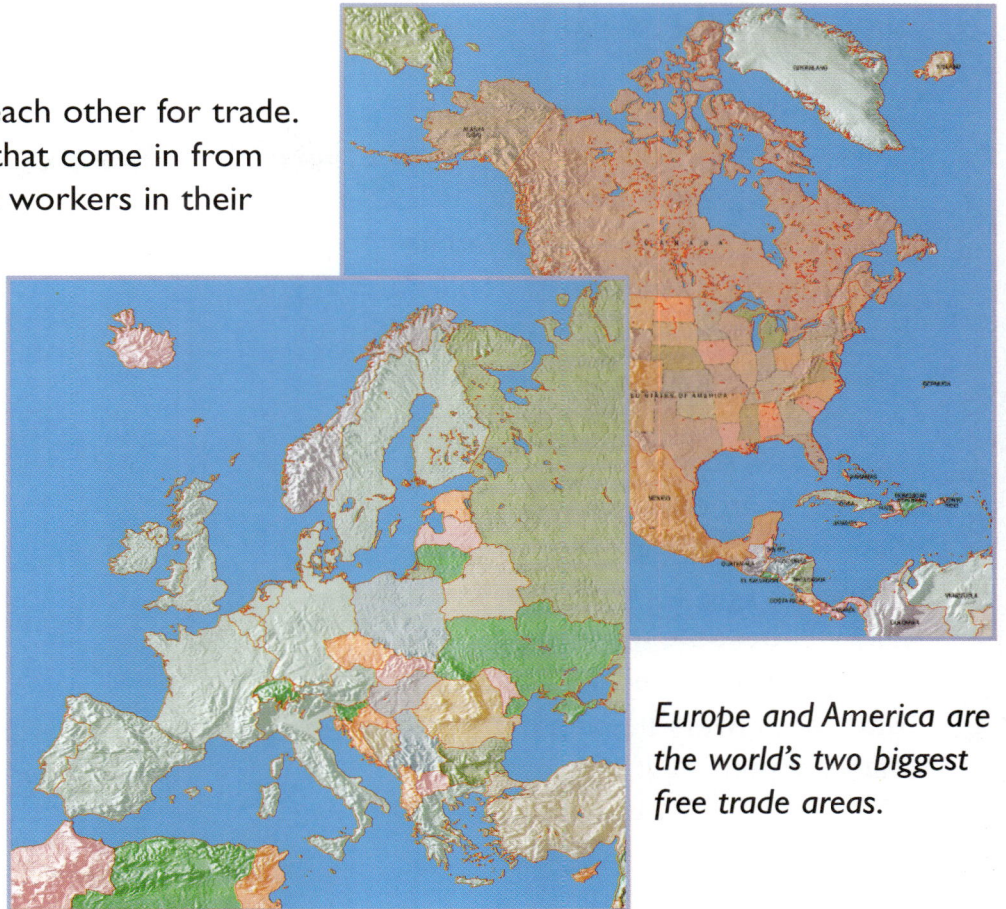

*Europe and America are the world's two biggest free trade areas.*

## Which is the world's oldest bank?

The Monte dei Paschi di Siena in Italy is the oldest bank in the world. It was established in 1472. It began as a charity pawn shop to provide interest-free loans to the poorest people. The bank is still in existence today, and now employs more than 28,000 people and has over 2,000 branches around Italy and the rest of the world.

## How do banks make money?

Banks make money in a variety of ways. When you deposit your money in a bank account the money is used by the bank to make more money. Banks lend this money to people and companies and charge interest on the loan so they get back more than they originally loaned. Banks also invest in stocks and shares which they hope will go up in value. In addition to this, banks also trade money. They buy money in one currency hoping that this will become more valuable compared to other currencies. This does not always happen but because banks spread their risk over many different sources they normally make a profit.

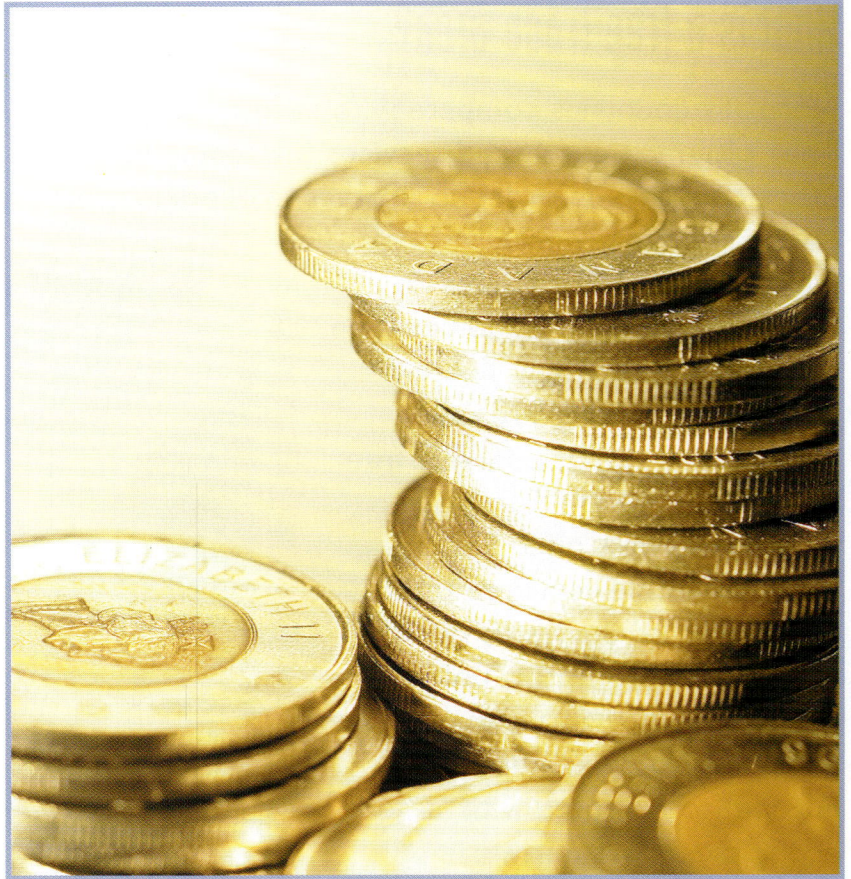

## What is a pyramid scheme?

A pyramid scheme is just one of the many get-rich-quick schemes that people think will make them money with little or no effort. Like all good scams they sound good in theory, but never work in practice. In a pyramid scheme a small number of initial participants get friends or colleagues to invest in some product or service. The profit comes from selling to people below you on the chain. These people in turn get other people to invest and the money goes up the chain in greater and greater amounts. Pyramid schemes always fail because no new money is created, only lost to other participants in the scheme. There is also a finite number of people prepared to invest in any pyramid scheme and this is soon reached causing the scheme to collapse. Pyramid schemes are illegal in nearly every country in the world.

# Which is the world's largest company?

The largest company in the world is the American grocery chain Wal-Mart Stores. Wal-Mart was started in 1962 by Sam Walton who opened his first store in Rogers, Arkansas. It has grown, in only 40 years, to the position of world number one with annual sales of $220 billion. Behind Wal-Mart are the more traditional global giants, the oil companies. The biggest of these, ExxonMobil has revenues of $191 billion. BP (British Petroleum) is the biggest non-American company in the world with annual revenues of $174 billion. Ford is the world's largest motor company with $162 billion in revenue. If you judge by profit, the world's most successful company is ExxonMobil which made $22 billion profit in 2003.

## What is a brand?

Brands are used by companies to identify themselves to consumers. They are created by a combination of advertising, packaging, public relations and word of mouth.

When people are choosing what to buy, the brand is one of the most powerful factors in influencing their choice. Someone looking to buy a BMW car is unlikely to choose a Ford instead, as the BMW brand is one they aspire to. Customers are very loyal to brands that they know and trust as is shown by the rivalry between the two computer companies, Apple and Microsoft. Buyers of Apple computers identify with the product they purchase. This makes it easier to sell other branded products to consumers. The world's most valuable brand is Coca-Cola, followed by Microsoft.

# Art and Literature

Art and literature is the embodiment of the human spirit. From scratches on cave walls to computer art, art shows us ourselves at our best and worst.

## How did ancient people create cave art?

Cave art dates back from 40,000 to 10,000 BC. Animals such as deer, the woolly mammoth and woolly rhinoceros, geometric shapes and humans were the most common shapes created. The first art was finger drawings using soft clay. This was followed by engraving on rock using sharp flint or stone picks. They also engraved the clay on cave floors, but much of this has been worn away by modern visitors. The final step in cave art was paintings that were created using colours from natural materials such as soil (red), kaolin (white) and burnt juniper or pine (black). Ancient artists even mixed colours together to create new colours.

## Which artist cut off his own ear?

Vincent van Gogh was a painter who was born in Holland in 1837. The emotional and troubled painter suffered from epilepsy and depression. After an argument with the artist Gauguin, van Gogh cut off part of his own ear. He was a painter for only ten years and his best works were produced in the last 2½ years of his life. He shot himself at the age of 37, dying in the arms of his beloved brother. Van Gogh sold only one of his paintings while he was alive.

## What is pointillism?

Pointillism is a type of painting where tiny dots of primary colours are used to create secondary colours. Pictures are created using the tiny dots of colour. The dots blend together when looked at from a distance. It is thought that mixing colours before you paint with them dulls them, therefore, pointillism is thought to produce brighter pictures. Pointillism was developed by the French painter Georges Seurat in the 1880s. One famous painting 'Sunday in the park' by Seurat has around 3.5 million dots and took two years to paint.

## Which famous sculpture did Michelangelo create?

The Statue of David was sculpted by Michelangelo Buonarroti. It was commissioned in 1501 and Michelangelo was given a large block of marble to create his statue with. David was a biblical king, who slew the giant Goliath. Michelangelo depicts David before the battle with Goliath. The statue is 4.34m tall and took three years to complete. It is considered one of the most beautiful art works ever. The statue was placed in the town square of the city of Florence in Italy. It became a symbol of strength and willingness to fight for the people. Michelangelo is also famous for painting the ceiling of the Sistine Chapel in the Vatican.

## Who painted the Mona Lisa?

The famous painting, the 'Mona Lisa' was painted by Leonardo da Vinci. It is the portrait of a woman from Florence, Mona Lisa, who was married to a nobleman, Francesco del Giocondo. Mona Lisa was del Giocondo's third wife, and she was 24 years old when he asked Leonardo to paint her. The painting took four years to complete, but it was never sold to del Giocondo. It is said that Leonardo loved the painting so much that he kept it for himself. He eventually sold it to King Francis I of France. The Mona Lisa now hangs in the Louvre museum in Paris.

## What is modern art?

Modern art is a name given to most of the art produced in Europe and America in the 20th Century, up until around 1970. (Art produced after this is known as contemporary art). Art is made not only from traditional materials but also any other material available, such as plastic and metal. Much of the art is abstract, where it does not look like what it is meant to be. Many 'new' methods of producing art are used in modern art, such as photography and printing. The industrial revolution influenced the creation of modern art.

# Is it art?

Contemporary art is the art of our times, just as the paintings of the great masters were contemporary in their days. Contemporary artists

work in a wide variety of mediums. As well as painting on canvas there are sculptors using wood, clay and metals as well as cloth, rubbish, and any number of other materials. Some artists work using film and video while others create art from found objects. It can be hard to understand some contemporary art as it is very different to that

which most people associate with art. This leads people to question whether it is art or not. The artist Carl Andre created a sculpture called Equivalent VIII which was a pile of 120 house bricks arranged into a shape. There was much public outcry at spending public money on art like this. Early Renaissance artists often received a similar reaction as did modern artists such a Miro and Picasso. All these artists are now accepted as great. Often with art, the public need time to accept new ideas. It is also important to educate people how to view art. In Leonardo da Vinci's day even the common people knew how to look at art and visited galleries. Nowadays people are exposed to very little art and visit art galleries in much fewer numbers.

# Who was Salvador Dali?

Salvador Dali was born in Figueras in Spain in 1904. He was a surrealist artist – his art showed images from the subconscious mind. His early paintings were of a dream world where objects were changed or grew in strange ways. He described his pictures as 'hand-painted dream photographs'. Later his style of painting became more traditional and his paintings were often on religious themes. Dali died from heart failure in 1989.

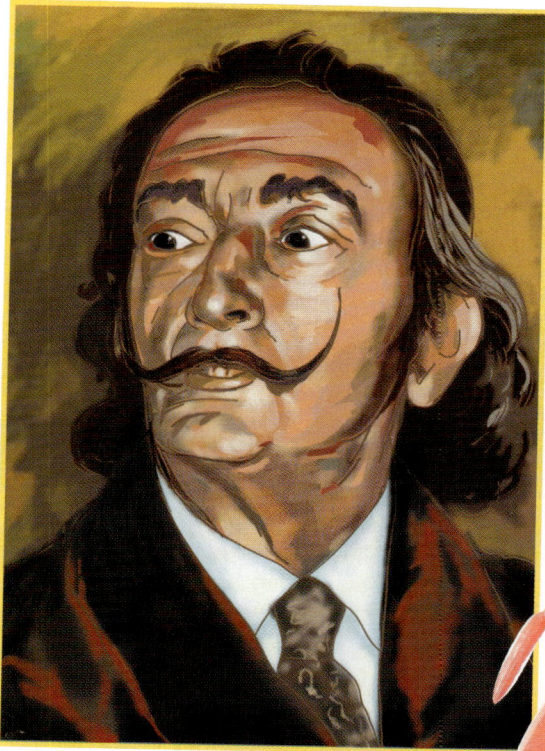

The 20th Century saw an explosion in various forms of art as artists tried to find new ways to interpret the world around them.

## Cubism
Principal artist Pablo Picasso. Picasso developed what he called cubism around 1906, along with Georges Braque. Cubism looks at objects from a variety of angles and seeks to represent the truth of the subject by showing it from multiple angles at the same time, distorting perspective and depth.

## Futurism
Principal artist Giacomo Balla. The Futurists strove to sweep away all that had gone before. They glorified speed, violence and technology. Futurism was short-lived but spawned Vorticism and Surrealism.

## Abstract expressionism
Principal artist Mark Rothko. A non-figurative art form that relied on colour and form to communicate intense emotions to the viewer, rather than depict a scene or conventional image.

## Pop Art
Principal artist Andy Warhol. Pop art was rooted in contemporary culture. Artists took commonplace visual imagery such as soup can labels and comic book panels and gave them new meaning by placing them in new contexts.

## Post-impressionism
Principal artist Paul Cézanne. Using vibrant colours and stylised brushstrokes these artists tried to convey both the visual and emotional form with equal importance.

# Who said 'I choose a block of marble and chop off whatever I don't need'?

These words were said by the French sculptor, Auguste Rodin, who was born in Paris in 1840. He attended art school from the age of 14. One of his most famous sculptures was 'Man with a broken nose'. Another of his works, 'The age of bronze', caused an uproar because it was so life-like that people couldn't believe that Rodin hadn't used a live model to cast it. This is something that no true sculptor would ever have done. This made Rodin more famous than any praise of his work could have, and brought in more work for him. Rodin died in 1917. He also produced one of the most famous sculptures in the world, 'The thinker'.

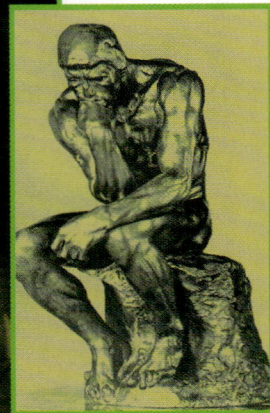

## Who was Andy Warhol?

Andy Warhol was an American artist and film maker who was born in 1928. During the 1960s he produced art from everyday items and products. He created identical pictures in different colours such as 'Campbell's Soup Cans' and 'Coca-Cola'. He also used famous people such as Marilyn Monroe and Elvis Presley. He tried to create art that appealed to ordinary people using themes from the culture at the time. This was known as pop art (popular art). Warhol died in 1987 after an operation.

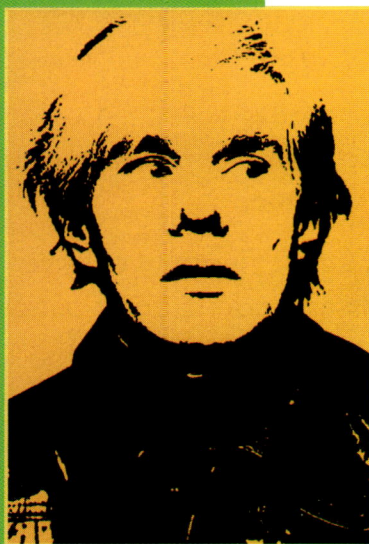

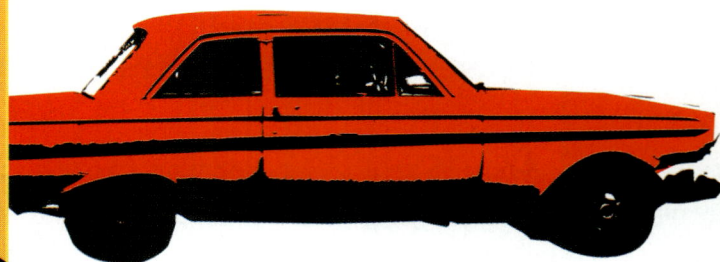

## Who was William Shakespeare?

Shakespeare was born in Stratford-upon-Avon in 1564. He grew up to become the most important playwright and author in the English language. He wrote his works between 1588 and 1616. His works include the plays Macbeth, Hamlet, The Merchant of Venice and Romeo and Juliet. He also wrote many short poems called sonnets. His works have been translated into every major language in the world and are still performed today on stages everywhere. There are also many film and TV adaptations of his works. He became director of his own theatre called the Globe, which was in Bankside in London. Shakespeare died in 1616. There is some dispute over who actually wrote some of his plays, but no one has been able to prove that he didn't, or that anyone else did.

## Which is the world's most read book?

The most popular book in the world is the Bible. It has been translated into virtually every world language. The current count stands at just over 2,600 languages, compared to the 50 or so that Shakespeare has managed. The Bible contains 39 Old Testament books and 27 New Testament books. The various books and psalms of the Bible were written over a period of around 1,500 years. The oldest book, the Book of Job was started in 1500 BC. The newest book, the Book of Revelations, tells of the end of the world and was written in 95 AD.

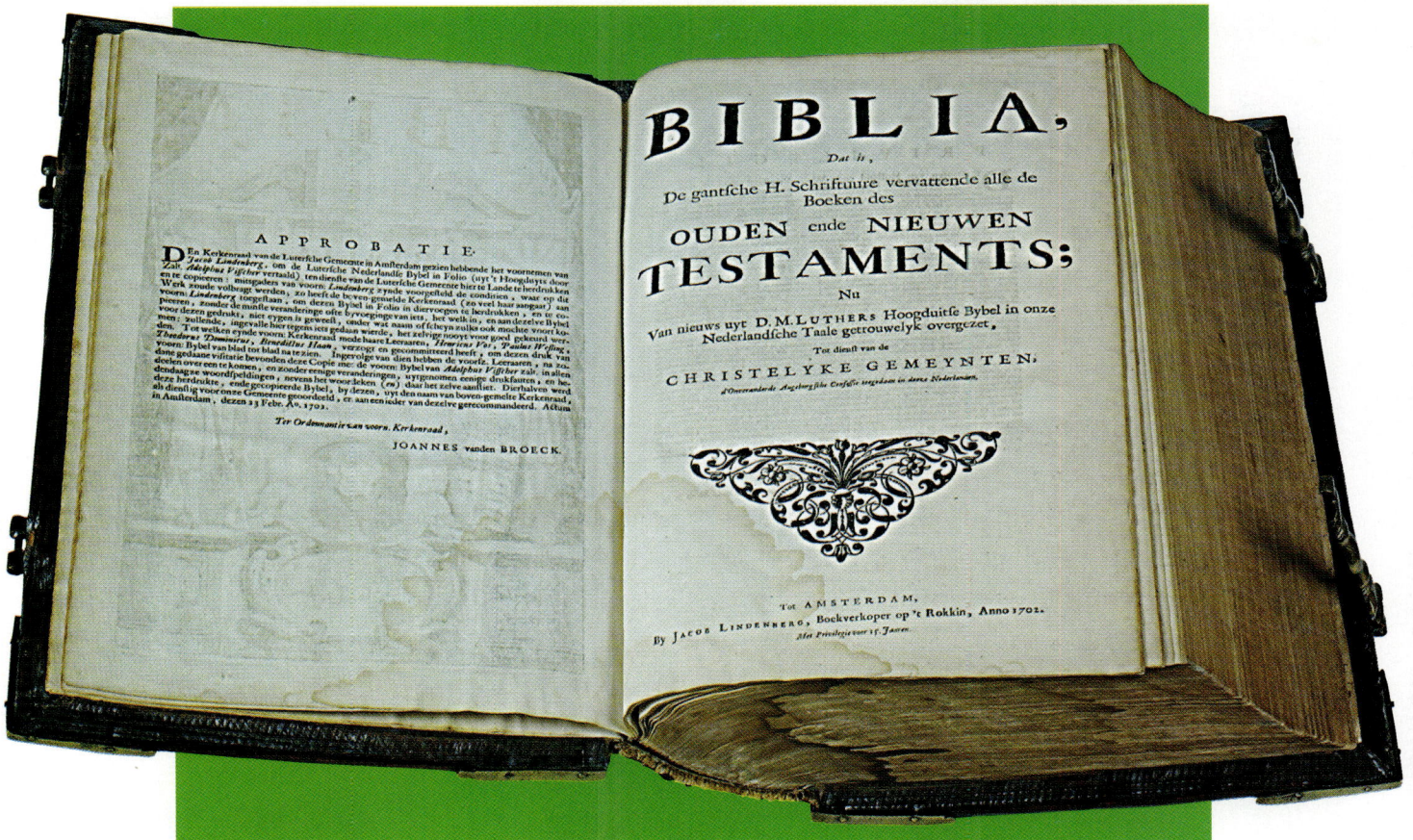

## Who was Mary Shelley?

Mary Shelley was the wife of the famous English poet Percy Shelley. She was also a famous novelist in her own right. Mary Shelley wrote Frankenstein, or The Modern Prometheus, its full title, for a bet when challenged to write a ghost story. She invented what is now the Gothic form of writing. Mary Shelley died in 1851. She was an early vegetarian and stood up for animal rights. The monster in her book was also a vegetarian. Over the years people have confused the identity of the Monster with that of Dr Frankenstein, who created it. In the book Dr Frankenstein was the real monster while the Monster was capable of great love and compassion.

*Shelley and her greatest creation, the Monster from Frankenstein.*

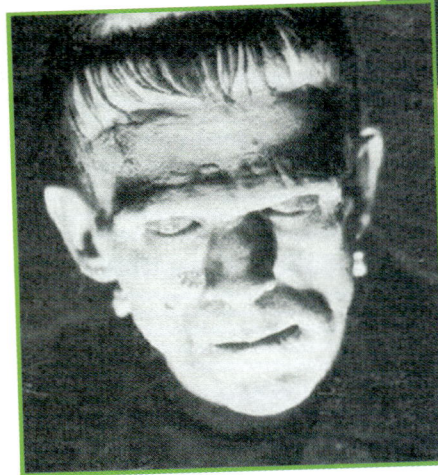

## What is street art?

Street art is, as the name implies, the art of the street. It started out as simple graffiti in the form of words and symbols. Competition between different street artists to create the most distinctive tags, as name symbols are known, led to the painting of more and more involved pieces. Soon people were commissioning street artists to create work for them instead of painting it onto public property. Street art is sometimes viewed as nothing more than graffiti, but the best of it reflects real life and the concerns of the people that live in run-down urban areas.

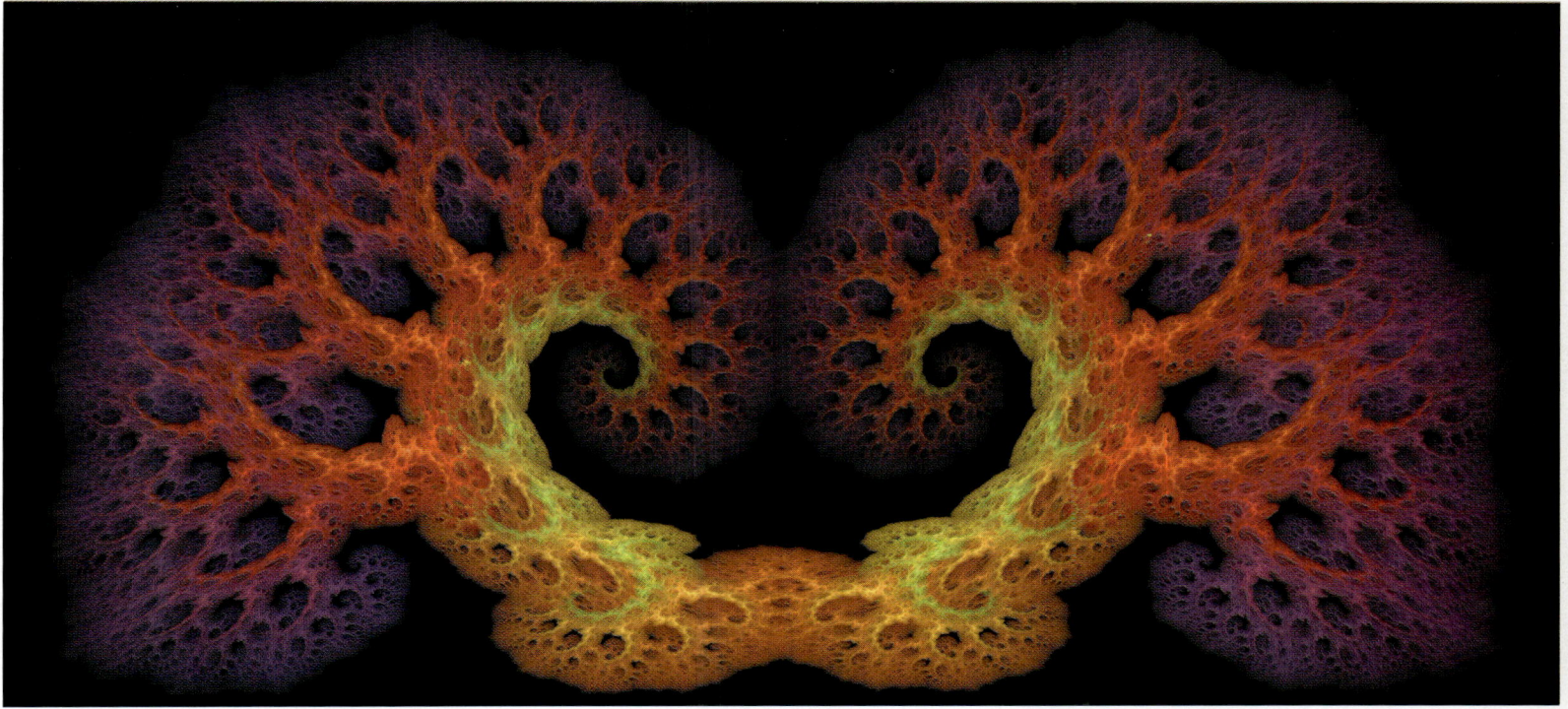

# What is computer art?

Computers are part of every aspect of our lives these days and art is no exception. Computer art can be divided into two main forms. That which uses a computer to visualise forms created by an artist, is often called cgi (computer graphics images). With cgi the artist is in control and decides how the art will look. The other form of computer art is in many ways more interesting. This uses complex mathematical formulae that the computer represents visually. The end image is not controlled by the artist but is the computer's response to billions of mathematical calculations. Some of the most famous images generated this way are the fractal images generated by the mathematics of chaos theory. These appeal to people because they represent underlying physical aspects of our universe in visual form.

# What is primitive art?

Primitive art is the art of indigenous cultures such as the native Americans, the Inuit and the Polynesian tribes of the South Pacific. Artists such as Picasso and Cézanne became interested in primitive art because they saw it as pure and unspoilt by the concerns of the modern world. They decided that it must, therefore, be closer to the 'truth' than decadent western art. Cézanne spent many years in the South Pacific studying the art there and Picasso was strongly influenced by African art. Today such art is prized by collectors, but there is a conflict between the local cultures who wish to retain their art and the rich investors who seek to remove it for display in galleries in the West.

# Glossary

**Ancestor**  An ancestor is a person from whom you are descended, normally more remote than grandparents. In many parts of the world, ancestors are especially respected and even worshipped.

**Atomic Bomb**  An atomic bomb is a bomb whose explosive power comes from the fission of heavy atomic nuclei. Two atomic bombs were dropped in World War Two at Nagasaki and Hiroshima, Japan, which effectively ended this war.

**Aborigine**  An Aborigine is a person that inhabits or exists in a land from the earliest times, or from before the arrival of colonists. It usually relates to a member of one of the indigenous peoples of Australia. The word aborigine comes from the Latin *ab origine* meaning 'from the beginning'.

**Amalgam**  An amalgam is a mixture or blend, such as mercury with another metal used by dentists for fillings.

**Assassination**  The deliberate murder of a person for political or financial gain.

**Bankrupt**  Having no money and being unable to pay your creditors.

**Commodity**  A commodity is anything that can be bought or sold, such as a raw material or an agricultural product.

**Currency**  The generic term for money of any sort.

**Descendant**  A person who is directly descended from a person of a previous generation or series of generations.

**Diversity**  Diversity is a varied range: the state of being varied. The word diversity comes from the Latin *diversus* meaning 'to turn aside'.

**Embodiment**  An embodiment is a concrete form of an abstract idea, such as a building could be the embodiment of an idea of an architect. The word comes from the Latin *fabricare* meaning 'to make or forge'.

**Endangered**  Driven to the brink of extinction by environmental pressures, including the effects of human activities.

| | |
|---|---|
| **Environment** | The environment is all the external factors that might surround and affect a person, animal or plant. These factors may be other living things or something non-living, such as amount of rainfall, the temperature or noise levels. |
| **Festival** | A day of celebration, often occurring annually and of a religious or spiritual nature. |
| **Grindstone** | A flat circular stone of natural sandstone that turns on an axle and is used for grinding, shaping or smoothing. |
| **Guerilla** | A soldier in a non-regular army who fights from concealment, often without wearing a uniform or other insignia. |
| **Haemorrhagic** | If something is haemorrhagic, it has blood escaping from a ruptured blood vessel. The word haemorrhage comes from the Greek *haima* meaning 'blood' and *rhegnunai* meaning 'burst'. |
| **Hypothermia** | A medical condition brought about by exposure to extreme cold. The body's core temperature becomes reduced and unconsciousness follows. Death will quickly result unless the body temperature can be raised. |
| **Invest** | To place money in a scheme or financial plan with the expectation of an increased return. The amount of additional money returned is governed by the interest rate. |
| **Manufacturing** | The production of goods through industrial or mechanised means. |
| **Mathematician** | A person who specialises in the solving of problems through mathematics. |
| **Nervous System** | The nervous system is the network of nerve cells and fibres, consisting of the brain, spinal cord, and nerves, which transmits nerve impulses between parts of the body. |
| **Nomadic** | A nomadic person is a member of a tribe that moves from place to place in search of food or pasture for its cattle. |
| **Paralysis** | An inability to control or move the muscles of the body. Most paralysis is of the voluntary muscles which allows continued breathing but nerve toxins paralyse the involuntary muscles, including the heart, resulting in death by suffocation. |

| | |
|---|---|
| **Philosopher** | A person who concerns themselves with the solution to moral and ethical problems through thought and the application of ideas. |
| **Polygamy** | Polygamy is the practice or condition of having more than one wife at the same time. It is illegal now in most parts of the world. |
| **Religion** | Religion is the belief in and worship of God or gods. |
| **Rennet** | A preparation made from the stomach lining of animals such as sheep and goats used in the process of curdling milk for cheese making. |
| **Ritual** | A ritual is a form or system of rites. The rites of baptism, marriage and burial are parts of the ritual of the Church. |
| **Sculpture** | A branch of art that deals with the exploration of three dimensional form, either in a figurative manner or using abstract forms. |
| **Symbolic** | Using symbols to represent an object or idea. Symbolism uses familiar objects or ideas to represent and help to explain more complex or intangible ideas. |
| **Synthetic** | Artificially produced. While the constituents of synthetic fibres are ultimately produced from natural products, they are differentiated from natural fibres such as wool or cotton. |
| **Tax** | A financial levy, on money earnt, that finances the governance of a country or region. |
| **Traditional** | Using methods and practices that have been passed down from generation to generation via word of mouth or written tradition. |
| **Worship** | To worship is to express or feel adoration or reverence for a god or goddess. |
| **Zodiac** | An imaginary band in the sky divided into different sections. The zodiac is used by astrologers to help them foretell future events for people based on the position of the stars on their individual birthday. |